VIOLENCE IN POP CULTURE

Published in the United States of America by Cherry Lake Publishing
Ann Arbor, Michigan
www.cherrylakepublishing.com

Content Adviser: Jessica Haag, MA, Communication and Media Studies
Reading Adviser: Cecilia Minden, PhD, Literacy expert and children's author

Photo Credits: ©sezer66/Shutterstock.com, Cover, 1; ©Vlasov Volodymyr/Shutterstock.com, 5; ©Lisette van der Kroon/Shutterstock.com, 6; ©Fernando Cortes/Shutterstock.com, 7; ©StockphotoVideo/Shutterstock.com, 8; ©KatsiarynaKa2/Shutterstock.com, 9; ©InesBazdar/Shutterstock.com, 10; ©Dragon Images/Shutterstock.com, 13; ©imtmphoto/Shutterstock.com, 15; ©Bornfree/Shutterstock.com, 16; ©REDPIXEL.PL/Shutterstock.com, 19; ©ALPA PROD/Shutterstock.com, 20; ©Monkey Business Images/Shutterstock.com, 21; ©wavebreakmedia/Shutterstock.com, 22; ©Tinxi/Shutterstock.com, 25; ©Victoria Lipov/Shutterstock.com, 27; ©Grzegorz Czapski/Shutterstock.com, 28

Library of Congress Cataloging-in-Publication Data

Names: Mara, Wil, author.
Title: Violence in pop culture / Wil Mara.
Description: Ann Arbor : Cherry Lake Publishing, [2018] | Series: Global citizens: modern media | Includes bibliographical references and index.
Identifiers: LCCN 2018005803 | ISBN 9781534129283 (hardcover) | ISBN 9781534130982 (pdf) | ISBN 9781534132481 (pbk.) | ISBN 9781534134188 (hosted ebook)
Subjects: LCSH: Violence in popular culture—Juvenile literature.
Classification: LCC HM1116 .M3695 2018 | DDC 303.6—dc23
LC record available at https://lccn.loc.gov/2018005803

Cherry Lake Publishing would like to acknowledge the work of the Partnership for 21st Century Learning. Please visit www.p21.org for more information.

Printed in the United States of America
Corporate Graphics

ABOUT THE AUTHOR

Wil Mara has been an author for over 30 years and has written more than 100 educational titles for children. His books have been translated into more than a dozen languages and won numerous awards. He also sits on the executive committee for the New Jersey affiliate of the United States Library of Congress. You can find out more about Wil and his work at www.wilmara.com.

TABLE OF CONTENTS

CHAPTER 1

History:
The Allure of
Violence

People have been communicating with each other for thousands of years. What began as rock carvings has slowly changed into books, newspapers, magazines, movies, radio, TV, and the Internet. Together, they are called **media**.

The media is a powerful tool. It can shape how people perceive the world around them. **Popular culture**, or pop culture, is connected to the media. It can influence people from how they dress to what movie they watch. Violence has become a

Some studies show that popular music lyrics have become more shocking over the years.

part of pop culture. And with the rise of the Internet and social media, we are exposed to violence on a daily basis. We hear it in popular songs on the radio. We watch it in movies and on television shows. It's in the video games we play. People are fascinated by it. As long as this attraction to violence remains the case, there will be some form of media ready to **broadcast** or publish it.

Ancient Rome used the Colosseum, or amphitheater,
to present brutal events for over 500 years.

Some historians estimate that there might have been close to 5,000 people killed every year during ancient Rome's violent games.

Ancient Times

It's easy to blame modern media for putting violent **content** into our homes. But people were drawn to violence long before social media, the Internet, and reality TV existed. In ancient Rome (753 BCE–476 CE), people gathered in an **amphitheater** to watch fights. Slaves, prisoners, and gladiators would fight before cheering crowds. Body padding and mouth guards were not used. It was a battle to the death.

Jousting tournaments became so popular during medieval times that knights would travel far distances to compete.

Middle Ages

The public hunger for violent entertainment continued after the fall of the Roman Empire in 476 CE. During the Middle Ages (476–1453 CE), jousting was a popular sport. Two men on horses would ride toward each other at great speed carrying a long, pointed pole, or lance. Their aim was to knock each other off their horse. The sport was meant as war training for medieval knights, but it also served to entertain spectators.

Hunting was a popular sport for both men and women during the Middle Ages.

Studies show that younger children are more likely to imitate violent acts they see on TV if they watch a "good guy" use violence to solve an issue.

Extra! Extra! Read All About It!

The invention of the **printing press** during the mid-1400s made it easier to expose people to violent content. Early publishers discovered that articles featuring violent passages sold well. From the mid-1500s to early 1700s, true crime reports were being published. These short reports soon turned into longer passages and then into published books. Readers enthusiastically welcomed these grim books into their home libraries.

Power of Modern Media

Media today has greater power and influence than ever before. For the first time in history, people on different sides of the world can connect with each other in seconds. While this technology has its advantages, it also has its disadvantages. The Internet, social media, and television can be used to spread violent content. Content shared online can go viral. Even children's cartoons show violence. Studies show that cartoons will depict at least 20 acts of violence in any given hour. By the age of 18, the average person will have seen over 200,000 acts of violence on television!

Developing Questions

There are many ways for children, teenagers, and adults to access violent content. Television, computers, tablets, smartphones, and movies make it easy and instant. With this in mind, do you think there needs to be a limit to how much violent content we consume? Why or why not?

CHAPTER 2

Geography: Pop Culture Violence the World Over

Pop culture has the power to influence a society. Sometimes one country's pop culture can dominate or influence that of another country. Most people would say that American pop culture takes the lead. Its influence is seen across different media types, from music to television shows to **blockbuster** movies. What about other countries?

Karaoke in the Philippines

Karaoke is a core part of Filipino pop culture. But a strange thing started happening in karaoke bars there in the early 2000s. The popular song "My Way" by Frank Sinatra led to at least

Karaoke-related violence also happens in other countries, like Malaysia, China, Thailand, and the United States.

six deaths and over a dozen injuries from fights. According to reports, the deaths and injuries occurred for various reasons. Some say the lyrics, like the line "I did it my way," brings up feelings of arrogance in the singer. This could be the reason it leads to fights. Others say because the song is picked more often than other karaoke songs, there is bound to be more violent acts associated with it. These violent acts would occur after breaking "karaoke etiquette," like not waiting your turn, hogging the microphone, or joining someone else's performance without being asked. The "My Way Killings," as they are commonly called, shook the country so much that the classic song was officially banned from all karaoke bars.

Computer and Video Games in China

China has traditionally kept a tight rein on what type of pop culture material reaches its citizens. From 2000 to 2014, it banned all video game consoles and the games played on them that weren't made in China. But even with the ban lifted, the games being sold still need to be approved. Two groups approve what is published and distributed to Chinese citizens. They are the China Audio-Video Copyright Association (CAVCA) and Ministry of Culture of the People's Republic of China (MOC). CAVCA and MOC determine what artists can perform, what content can be broadcast on the radio or television, and what users can search and view on the Internet.

CAVCA also decides what computer and video games citizens can play. For instance, *PlayerUnknown's Battlegrounds* was one of the top online games of 2017. The realistic game features characters who must defend themselves, sometimes using weapons that look real. CAVCA issued a statement claiming that the game goes against China's values and culture, so it will most likely be

In 2013, 24 percent of mobile gamers in China were 10 to 19 years old.

banned. However, this doesn't mean all violent games are banned in China. *Honor of Kings*, a top-selling game in China, features violent content. But because the characters and weapons aren't realistic, it isn't banned.

Violence in Iceland

Iceland is known to be one of the happiest countries in the world, teenagers included. It is also known as one of the safest countries. According to the Global Peace Index, Iceland has ranked number one as the safest and most peaceful country every year since 2008. Interestingly, tourism is booming in Iceland because of violence in American pop culture. *Game of Thrones*, a popular American television show, depicts excessive violence using Iceland as one of the backdrops. Iceland was also a setting for the violent American movies *Prometheus* (2012) and *Star Wars: The Force Awakens* (2015). It has been reported that in 2016, over 2.4 million tourists visited Iceland—a country with a little over 300,000 citizens!

Gathering and Evaluating Sources

Numerous studies show that violence in pop culture can negatively influence children and young adults. Despite this, some experts believe the opposite. They argue that the violence in pop culture helps young adults define their own moral boundaries. They believe that reading books and watching movies, like the Hunger Games trilogy, are beneficial. They can help young adults cope with their own emotions. Do you agree? Why or why not? Use the information found in this book and resources found at your local library to support your answers.

Civics: The Effect on People

Violence in pop culture has an effect on people. Almost everyone agrees on this. What many researchers and psychologists can't seem to agree on is how much it affects people. And is the impact negative or positive?

Video Games

Video games have been part of pop culture from Japan to Argentina to the United States. Over 90 percent of American children and young adults play video and computer games. About 85 percent of those games are violent. Some studies claim that after playing violent video games, children tend to act more

In the United States, 65 percent of homes have at least one person playing 3 hours or more of video games a week.

aggressively. This led to the formation of the Entertainment Software Rating Board (ESRB) in 1994. The ESRB created ratings for video games, from EC (Early Childhood) to M (Mature).

In addition, President Barack Obama established the American Psychological Association Task Force in 2013. Its goal was to go through all the research on violence in video games and determine whether it affected behavior. The conclusion was that there is a link to short-term aggressive behavior. However, there is no real link between playing violent video games and criminal behavior.

In the United States, 41 percent of video gamers are women.

According to a study, all G-rated animated movies made in the United States between 1937 and 1999 featured violence.

Television and Movies

Television and movies are also a big part of pop culture. Several studies have been done looking for a link between violent TV and movies and their effect on children. But most studies are almost 20 years old! One of the more recent studies from 2010 found that children and young adults ages 8 to 18 spent about 4 hours every day watching television. Around 60 percent of TV shows included violent acts, with an average of six violent acts per hour.

According to Apple, its video streaming platform will focus on comedies and heartfelt dramas and won't feature violence or strong language.

...udy was done in the mid-1990s. It found that

...avior among children rose from around 3 percent

...5 percent after they watched a violent TV show.

...vent even higher after watching a violent full-length

...study noted that about 40 percent of the top G- and

...nimated movies featured characters carrying a gun.

Developing Claims and Using Evidence

...day is very different than it was 10 years ago.

...e different than pop culture in the 1920s, 1960s,

...ow violence is portrayed in pop culture is also

...g the library and the Internet, research violence in

...om different decades. How has it changed? Do you

...ence portrayed is worse, better, or the same? Use the

...find from your research to support your claims.

CHAPTER 4

Economics: The Business of Violence

Many businesses make money off pop culture trends. Sometimes these trends feature dark themes. Because violence is part of pop culture and attracts people, it's no surprise that businesses feature these dark themes.

It Pays to Play

Around the world, there are roughly 2.2 billion gamers. It is estimated that they earned the video game industry $108.9 billion in 2017. In 2016, the earnings were only a little over $100 billion. That's about an 8 percent increase in **revenue**! Surprisingly,

Some professional gamers make as much as $150,000 a year!

China took the lead despite its strict rules on video games. It made about $27.5 billion in video game sales, which accounts for about 25 percent of the world market. Most of this money was made from violent video games.

In the United States, 27.5 percent of video games sold in 2016 were shooter games. Action games came in a close second, with 22.5 percent of games being sold. The top three best-selling video games that same year were all rated M (Mature).

The video game industry is so massive that it will be included in the 2022 Asian Games. eSports is organized video game competitions where players compete for cash. In 2022, these gamers will be able to compete for medals. If violence is kept to a minimum, eSports may be considered for the Olympic Games in the future.

Fashion and Music

Fashion, music, and pop culture have always gone hand in hand. When one thing is trending in the world of music, it most certainly crops up in the fashion people wear. According to a study, 69 percent of people agree that a musician's style influences their own style. People also turn to them for style inspiration. Seventy-five percent women and 62 percent men turn to them more than any other type of celebrity. Furthermore, 60 percent of **Generation Z** and **millennials** say that their style and the brands they buy are heavily based on musicians they listen to.

Back in the 1960s, '70s, and early '80s, heavy metal was a core part of pop culture. This type of music typically featured death, violence, and other grim themes. Today, this music has made a comeback—at least in clothing form. Justin Bieber is one of the

Many fashion ads and window displays feature dark and violent themes
to help draw people into the store.

According to research, many adult-rated films have toy tie-ins that target children as young as 4 years old!

Taking Informed Action

Violence is everywhere, both in real life and in fiction. It's in the news. It's in movies, music, and video games. It's featured on the clothes we wear. Think about the last time you saw violence in pop culture. Was it from a music video or movie you just watched? Think about your favorite television show. Does it feature violence? If so, how often? The next time you go to the movies, take note of how many violent themes are featured. Do you think those themes were a necessary part of the movie? Why or why not? Check out a G-rated movie. Is there any form of violence featured?

world's top-earning celebrities, having made an estimated
$83.5 million in 2017. He has been seen sporting Metallica and
Iron Maiden shirts, popular metal bands in the 1970s and '80s.
He has shed his "good-boy" image for an edgier, more rebellious
look. And it's all because of another musician: Kanye West.

Around 2014, Kanye started wearing metal-inspired clothes.
His fans, both famous and not, did the same. A small, affordable
fashion label even got a boost in revenue from West. He was
seen wearing one of the label's sweatshirts, and the item sold
out almost immediately. Today, we see this metal-inspired style
everywhere, from fashion runways to Forever 21.

Communicating Conclusions

Before you read this book, did you know how common violent themes were in pop culture? Now that you know more about violence in pop culture, why do you think it's important to be aware of the content you see, hear, read, and wear? Share what you've learned with your friends and family. Ask them how aware they are of violence in pop culture.

Think About It

Violent content is also widespread on the Internet and social media. It may seem harmless, but sometimes it can lead to violence. In 2009, there was a Photoshop contest. One of the images, called *Slender Man*, went viral. Fictional stories about this mysterious being were written and posted on popular online forums. The character was referenced in the *Minecraft* video game and even generated its own video game which was downloaded over 2 million times. A YouTube video of a person playing the game was watched over 12 million times. Unfortunately, the creepy made-up character inspired real-life violence by young people. According to them, Slender Man told them to do the things they did.

Research indicates that children as young as 2 1/2 years old know the difference between reality and fiction. However, experts suggest that because the brain isn't fully developed until age 25, young people can make violent and impulsive decisions. Other experts suggest that repeated viewings of violence lead to an increase in aggression and **desensitization** to violence.

What do you think? Do young people tend to be more impulsive and violent than adults? Does watching violent content repeatedly make people more aggressive and numb to violence? Research this topic further using the Internet and the library. Use the information you find to support your reasoning.

For More Information

Further Reading

Gimpel, Diane Marczely. *Violence in Video Games.* Minneapolis: ABDO Publishing, 2013.

Roesler, Jill. *Asking Questions About Violence in Popular Culture.* Ann Arbor, MI: Cherry Lake Publishing, 2016.

Websites

KidsHealth—Are Video Games Bad for Me?
http://kidshealth.org/en/kids/video-gaming.html?WT.ac=k-ra#catout
Read more about whether video games are bad or good.

Smithsonian TweenTribune
https://www.tweentribune.com
Stay updated on what's trending in the world.

GLOSSARY

aggressively (uh-GRES-iv-lee) acting in a manner that threatens others

amphitheater (AM-fih-thee-uh-tur) a building with seats rising in curved rows around an open space on which games and plays take place

blockbuster (BLAHK-bus-tur) nickname for a movie that has higher-than-average success

broadcast (BRAWD-kast) made public by means of radio or television

content (KAHN-tent) material that forms the core of something and is expressed through some form of media

desensitization (dee-sen-sih-tuh-ZUY-shuhn) the act or process of reacting less or being less affected by something

Generation Z (jen-uh-RAY-shuhn ZEE) a group of people born from the mid-1990s to the early 2000s

karaoke (kar-ee-OH-kee) a form of entertainment in which a device plays the music of popular songs and people sing along to the songs they chose

media (ME-dee-uh) a method of communication between people, such as a newspaper

millennials (muh-LEN-ee-uhlz) people born from the early 1980s to mid-1990s

popular culture (PAHP-yuh-lur KUHL-chur) commercial products that reflect or are aimed at the tastes of younger people via mass media; also known as pop culture

printing press (PRINT-ing PRES) a device designed to print ink onto paper in large quantities

revenue (REV-uh-noo) the amount of money that is made from some investment

INDEX